AUTISTIC LEGENDS ALPHABET

Words by Robin Feiner

A is for Jessica-Jane **A**pplegate. Using swimming as an outlet for her unlimited energy, she tumble-turned her life around to become the first British S14 Paralympian to win Gold. She has also set multiple world records and even been awarded an MBE.

B is for Tim **B**urton.
As a child, he spent a lot of time painting, drawing and watching films. He turned his fantastic imagination into a legendary career as a filmmaker, with movies like 'Alice in Wonderland' and 'Corpse Bride' winning him a place in the hearts (and nightmares!) of millions.

C is for Corinne Duyvis. Little did this young Dutch trailblazer know that being diagnosed with autism would motivate her to dive into all of her passions. She became a published author, co-founded a blog called 'Disability in KidLit' and started the #ownvoices hashtag movement, all in the name of diversity.

D is for Dan Aykroyd. This multi-talented actor and comedian credits ASD for his obsessive interest in ghosts and law enforcement. He cheerfully acknowledges that without these fascinations, he would never have had the inspiration for his massive box-office hit, 'Ghostbusters.' Who you gonna call?

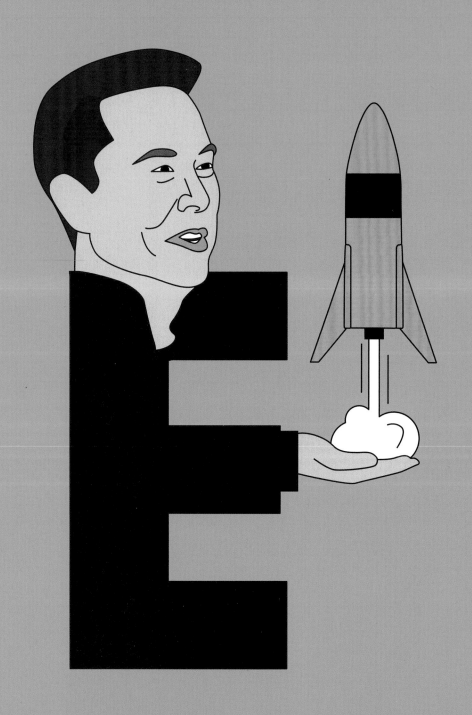

Ee

E is for **E**lon Musk.
When this tech billionaire announced he had Asperger's syndrome while hosting U.S. comedy sketch show 'Saturday Night Live,' he was met with loud cheers and applause. As the brains behind Tesla and SpaceX, this visionary has reinvented electric cars and will soon send us to Mars!

F is for Bobby **F**ischer. Becoming a chess grandmaster at age 15, Bobby's talent was evident from a young age. And when this 'Mozart of chess' defeated Russian, Boris Spassky, in 1972, he became the first American World Champion and an inspiration to a new generation of young players.

Gg

G is for Hannah **G**adsby. Feeling like she'd never quite fit in, this Australian comedian was officially diagnosed with ADHD and autism as an adult. In her groundbreaking Netflix stand-up specials, 'Nanette' and 'Douglas,' she sends a passionate message that neurodiversity is a normal part of life, and that "diversity is strength."

H is for Daryl **H**annah.
This star of legendary movies
like 'Blade Runner', 'Roxanne'
and 'Kill Bill' was for many
years a shy and introverted
young girl struggling with
borderline autism. But acting
gave her an escape from
herself, and she ended up
making quite a 'splash'
as a leading lady.

I is for Anthony Ianni.
He was diagnosed with PDD, bullied and told he'd never graduate high school let alone have a basketball career – but he never gave up. Graduating from college and winning two Big Ten Championships, he's now a motivational speaker for autism awareness and the fight against bullying.

J is for **J**odi DiPiazza. She's the 11-year-old musical prodigy who performed a duet of 'Firework' with Katy Perry – bringing six million people to tears and raising over four million dollars for autism education. Jodi is now studying music at college and continues to inspire at benefit concerts across the U.S.

Kk

K is for Heather Kuzmich.
She went on 'America's Next
Top Model' to test her limits.
And while her ASD sometimes
made her endearingly shy
and awkward in front of
the camera, her bravery in
going on the show won her
thousands of fans and helped
raise awareness of autism.

L is for Leslie Lemke. Battling blindness, brain damage and cerebral palsy, this savant had a rough start to life. After giving him a piano at age 7, his adoptive mother discovered he could play back music after hearing it only once. He became a musical virtuoso and toured Scandinavia, the U.S. and Japan!

M is for Barbara **M**cClintock. When told she had won the 1983 Nobel Prize for her work on 'jumping genes,' Dr. Barbara famously replied, "Oh dear," and went for a walk! Painfully shy, her ability to fixate on one particular topic undoubtedly helped in her time-consuming and thorough research.

Nn

N is for Jerry Newport. Diagnosed with ASD, this savant and mathematical genius could perform difficult calculations in his head. He married Mary Louise Meinel, also a savant with ASD, and together they wrote their heart-warming love story in 'Mozart and the Whale,' which was later made into a movie.

Oo

O is for Freddie **O**dom. Having autism didn't stop him from becoming an actor, author, teacher and independent politician. In fact, shortly after announcing his diagnosis, he was chosen as the Mayor of Bluffton, Georgia, and became the first known elected official with autism in U.S. history. Inspirational!

**P is for Pip Brown.
ASD made this Kiwi musician
so scared of going on stage
and interacting with her
audience that she even called
her 2012 album, 'Anxiety.'
Using 'Ladyhawke' as her
stage name helped Pip manage
her anxieties, and she now
enjoys rocking out with
her fans.**

Q is for Beauty **Q**ueen, Alexis Wineman. She overcame chronic shyness, speech impediments and bullying to become the first contestant with autism in a 'Miss America' pageant in 2013. Her credo, "Autism doesn't define me. I define it," is encouraging thousands of others with autism to follow their dreams.

R is for Rodaan Al Galidi. As an asylum seeker in the Netherlands, this Iraqi native wasn't allowed to attend language classes. So he taught himself to speak and write Dutch, and in 2011, his novel 'The Autist and the Carrier Pigeon' won the European Union Prize for Literature.

S is for Satoshi Tajiri.
His autism made him obsessed with trying to combine his two favorite passions: video games and collecting bugs. Finally, in 1996, with the help of Nintendo, this Japanese gamer's dream became a reality, and 'Pokémon,' the legendary 'collecting' video game, was born!

T is for Greta **T**hunberg. She insists she didn't become a climate change activist in spite of autism, but because of it. In fact, this teenage legend sees her ASD as a kind of superpower that allows her to hone in on the core issue of climate change and ignore irrelevant distractions.

U is for Ulysse Delsaux. Having autism gives this young French NASCAR driver a distinct edge during races: being able to shut out the rest of the world. Inspiring other sports people with autism, he's already won the Elite 2 Championship and is climbing the ladder in Elite 1. Young legend!

V is for Vernon L. Smith. This astoundingly-gifted professor credits autism, and the selective focusing and problem-solving abilities it gives him, as the secret weapon behind his 2002 Nobel Prize in behavioral economics. The Vernon Smith Center for Experimental Economics Research is named in his honor.

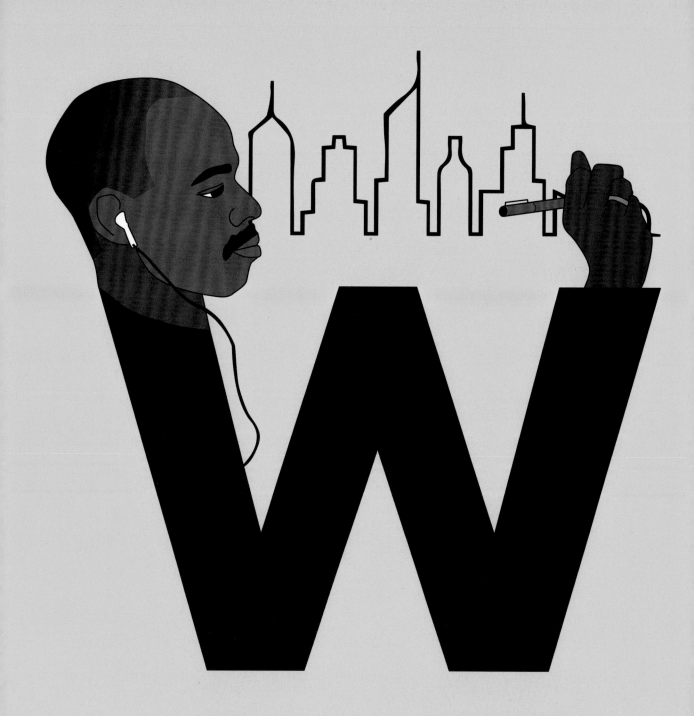

W is for Stephen **Wiltshire.** Nicknamed the 'human camera,' Stephen can see a city once then draw it in perfect detail, entirely from memory. Diagnosed with autism at age three, this internationally-acclaimed artist now has his own gallery and has been awarded an MBE for his services to art.

X is for The Autisti**X**.
You can have autism and still rock. That's the philosophy behind AutistiX, the legendary U.K. indie rock band with three members with autism in its lineup. While autism affects them each differently offstage, the moment the music starts, they become perfectly in sync and rock the house!

Yy

**Y is for Adam Young.
Describing himself as shy
and deeply introverted, the
'Owl City' front man spent
years conducting interviews
only by email. Conquering his
biggest fear of playing in front
of crowds, he's learnt how to
have a good time by losing
himself in the music.**

Zz

Z is for Jason **Z**immerman. While having autism can sometimes make it hard for this pro video gamer to socialize and communicate, 'Mew2King' reigns supreme with a console in his hand! Able to shut out all distractions thanks to his autism, 'The Robot' is one of the greatest gamers of all time.

The ever-expanding legendary library

EXPLORE THESE LEGENDARY ALPHABETS & MORE AT WWW.ALPHABETLEGENDS.COM

AUTISTIC LEGENDS ALPHABET
www.alphabetlegends.com

Published by Alphabet Legends Pty Ltd in 2021
Created by Beck Feiner
Copyright © Alphabet Legends Pty Ltd 2021

978-0-6486724-4-9

Printed and bound in China.